VENomoUS

VENomoUS

Say More with Less

Adeola Awe

Believe in what you can see.
Otherwise, you'll be deceived
by greedy thieves
who offer no reprieve.
Don't be fooled
by those fueled
by cruel-ty.
Unable to rule effectively.
Lacking the necessary tools
needed to effect change.
I find it strange
that we award them praise.
Raised to a state of our creation.
Infatuated by their weightless words
while ours remain unheard.
Their statements lack cement,
made evident by the state of affairs.
They could not care less
as displayed by their carelessness,
but we continuously invest.
Undeserving of our trust.
We must not allow our minds to rust
nor gather dust.
The alternative is rather disastrous.

Honeymoon phase
eyes glazed
cloudy judgement
shrouded in haze
behavior gazed over
concerns not raised
dazed and confused
abuse ensues.
How do you maneuver
through manure
whilst skewered?
Fueled by disdain,
spewing profanities
won't remedy the pain.
Exercise refrain
and abstain
from entertaining trains
that are bound to wreck.

Who's allowed to alter
my present state?
Permitted to degrade
and falter my gait?
Welcome to enter
my space
and displace me
from center?
Euthymia
proves to be a feat.
Glued to my seat,
outlook gloomy and bleak.
My feet carry me
from trough to peak,
unconditionally,
despite the lethargy,
making me weak.

Supplant sweet nothings
with something sweet
to ease the depleting feeling,
pleading for
the never-ending to cease.
My time will elapse
when a lapse of judgment
causes me to relapse
to past encounters
that counter
my future endeavors.
Forever stunted until confronted.
The result is less tumult-uous.
Fill the gaping hole,
so there's no escaping.
Bravely facing hurdles
before I hurtle
into a bout of hurt
I'd rather do without.
Lingering traces erased,
space replaced
with a sturdier base.
No longer perturbed.

I find it odd
that many applaud
frauds.

Maya dissolves.
Weight alleviates
the higher I evolve.
Enthralled,
I graduate from a crawl.
My hands push me to stand,
feet planted,
stance advances,
no cushion to break my fall.
Life at stake,
steps directed by The All.
Who's there to call
when almost all
are inanimate walls?
Wasted breath
brings death closer.
Instead of venting,
time could be better spent
implementing,
cementing
my own counsel.

Do you feel attacked
when shown areas of lack
you refuse to unpack?
Afraid of being pushed-back?
Would you rather
a pat on the back
or a smack?
Should I retract what I said,
so we can dead it here?
Steer clear of fears
you're unwilling to hear?

Time moves irrespective
of our measurements.
Never constrained.
Elapses not.
While we collapse
at the thought
that we ought
to do more.
Running on reserve
instead of preserving.
Fueled by drive.
Soon arrives the mess
we'll be forced to address
when the ripples
our actions create
leave us crippled,
in a lesser state.

It's better to be alone
than regress to those you've outgrown.

I cannot afford
to reward myself with discord.
Form chords to later sword
all because of boredom?
Step into spheres
when it's clear
that temptation lurks near?
Desire never tires
as time expires.
With sustained effort
less effort is required
to temper the fire
when the flesh is tempted
to choose death
without considering the breadth
of its choice.
Today, in the present.
Tomorrow, in resent
when its intent was well meant.
Short-lived pleasure never measures up
to the forever effects of the innate.
No input needed to satiate.
Delivers on its promise
with no slivers on its plate.

The job pays for a bill
but offers no thrill.
The monotony tires me,
expedites my expiry.
Not wanting either extreme
but something in-between
standing and scanning a screen.
The thing of dreams.
The best option I've found
leads to the ground,
covered in a mound
same way.
I pray for the day
I no longer weigh between
whether I should leave or stay
in hell when it's telling
that I should prioritize
alternate dwelling
when the latter is not compelling.

My belief offers relief
stronger than any doubt
that may have me reroute
to avoid drought.
Not wanting to starve
but unaware of the fated harvest
orchestrated by The Greatest Artist.
My forced hand
could never equate
to the grand plan
that awaits me.

Dread best describes the feeling
when your bread cannot be eaten.
No room for inconsequential non-essentials.
A one-to-one of income to expenses
is quite cumbersome.
If the unexpected befalls,
no net exists to catch the haul.
The feeling of powerlessness
is difficult to resist when it's persistent.
Despite my attempts to quiet my despair,
suspended in the air
a heavy weight has yet to alleviate.
Turbulence gives way to ease.
No queasy feeling,
head lifts from between my knees.
Drifting calmly above the sea below,
an anchor I throw
so as not to be thrust about by a gust.
The water's womb, a tomb for me
to develop in its enveloped cocoon.
The Moon illum-inates a path untraversed.
Not a second to rehearse for the worst
when beckoned.

Unsolicited critique
elicits a knee-jerk reaction
when it concerns my work.
Having to reason with those
less-seasoned
is like trying to temper a child.
Futile.
To obliterate the irritation,
don't seek the cause of your frustration.
Protect against harboring emotions
that dock and cause commotion
when they flock.
This level can be beat.
Don't succumb to defeat.
Guard against deplete
by retreating.
When compromise fails to result
and "to no avail" prevails,
realize that offering aid to an ailment
after failed attempts
is pointless.

If I refuse to accept a part,
would I be rejecting the whole?
Did it exist at the start
or form as a byproduct of evolutionary art?
Having to conform to an abnormal norm
leaves me torn.
"To exclude would be rude," they say,
but to include would cause internal feud.
Having to befriend and play pretend
to maintain face when faced with a complex
leaves perplex-ity in its wake.
Anyone can see through fakes
since they're not opaque.
A blank is drawn when no memory bank
can be called upon.
Confusion is oftentimes foreign
with alien origin.
Don't struggle to comprehend
when your efforts dead end.
If the pieces cannot be mended cohesively,
the puzzle may be defective.

Monstera is an unsuitable name
for such a tame plant.
Who cowers from a towering flower
that simply thirsts for a shower?
The earth has birthed far worst.
There are those who vacillate
between love and hate
and desert when dessert is no longer plated,
causing hurt instead of comfort
to those related.
Many possess a tenth of the strength
needed to loosen the grip of illusory trips.
Oftentimes, disease is caused by
pleasing things that bring
a false sense of ease,
seizing the body as its captive
while the mind remains captivated
by its captor,
caught in a merciless bind
anything but kind, unlike *Monstera*.

Self-harm to self-soothe;
the paradox is quite alarming.
Tasked to disarm my own hand
and stand up against the destructive force
coursing through my veins.
It's hard to refrain from inflicting pain
when it offers brief relief
and abates my conflicted state.
- a welcome reprieve from overwhelm -
The path will be made evident
but is now uncertain,
blacked out by a curtain.
My inner child
yearns to be wild,
free from distress,
yet met with oppress-ive force.
Forced to mature pre-maturely
and assume an all-encompassing role
with no compass,
attempting to navigate ship
but ill-equipped
to prevent the inevitable slip.

I've been conditioned to ignore
the roaring storm within my form,
providing me with a forewarn.
Whispers fail to disturb
unlike thunder, which can be heard
and felt as it reverbs.
Insides churn,
yearning for reprieve.
Ready to depart (i.e., leave)
when the art lacks heart
from the start.
Unable to wet my appetite,
yet I stomach another bite
despite.
Each successive
less delight-ful than the one prior.
In dire need of the hollow to be swallowed
by the fire,
so I can be devoid of this tire.
In sole (soul) pursuit of
what inspires me to strive higher.
No plummet from the summit
once I arrive.

Expending energy on trivial matters
instead of tending to those most important
will inevitably leave me scattered
and dampen my focus.
When my egoic identification
brings no elation,
I find I'm no longer defined
by the self-imposed bind
that's kept me confined for some time.
I must be reminded that
"all is mind."
First, you must admit
that you're neither forced nor coerced
to submit;
you can quit
if the shoe doesn't fit,
which is *not* synonymous with
lacking grit nor failing to commit.
Money is a cheap incentive
used by the insensitive
to keep one from choosing defiance
over compliance
when self-reliance is a viable option
and often, if not always, more reliable.

We wake up
when we choose to get out of bed.

Say More with Less

This project is dedicated to
those who have preceded me
and to those who will succeed me
and succeed indeed.

Less dense
I give utmost reverence
to Opulence.
The Essence
that lessens
the tension
and faultiness
of five-sense perception
of this experience.

A foundation cannot sustain
on uneven terrain.

How do you deprogram
when you're deep in the program?

.

Confront that which stunts.

Peel back the rind
to the core.
The sore truth ignored not.
No matter how por-ous
you may feel,
the veil no longer conceals
the hurt.
Birthed through pain,
the pleasure
immeasurable.
No longer tethered to whether
you should shoulder the burden
or remove the boulder altogether.
Start anew with an ace
not a trace of the distaste
stomached.

I'm playing a game
with no clear objective,
impartial to whether I win
or simply meet the bare min.
My limbs fatigued
from futile attempts to advance
against the current,
a deterrent,
pushing me toward a fut-ure
I can no longer re-fute
and away from a past
never intended to last.
Self-imposed torture
I refuse to endure
lest I mourn the loss
- opportunity cost -
of what could be
for the familiarity
of the present,
a transient gift
I've come to resent.

There's a part of me
unwilling to part
with a cultural script
that ought to be ripped to shreds
and laid to bed
lest I spend my waking hours
in dread,
blindly led and underfed.
Malnourished,
unable to flourish
into my final form.
Torn between an ideal
and a real-ity
born into and conformed.

I'm nearing the end of a time
where I cease to revere nor identify
with wants not inherently mine,
confined to another's storyline
unless I choose an alternate route—
better-suited
for my passionate pursuit
toward ripe fruit—
with no gripes nor rues
about what I should and should not do.
My Tower isn't structurally sound.
I'm found bare,
hyperaware,
scared of the turbulent ground.
"There's no need to be frightened,"
says the dark night.
"You have the keys to enlighten
and become One with The Light."

Don't condemn nor condone.
To each their own.

How does one interact
but not distract oneself from
the known fact
that most act
in order to catch contact?

Any opponent with intent to harm
will be disarmed.

You'll wreck
if you break your neck
to check
how far others have trekked.

Give no reactions to distractions.

Take time
to comb through
and prune.
Soon,
you'll fine-tune
your worldview
no longer misconstrued
by the news-ance.

I've gradually become
numb
to the humdrum
web of lies spun.
There's no air to vent
nor lament
about events designed
to prevent the Ascent.

Become less reliant
on the advice
others have acquired.
Confusion comes
when you admire
a choir.
Believe in your Power
that doesn't cower
behind material desire
laced in copper wire.
Trust that Source
will keep you on Course.
Withdraw from discourse
that is surface.
You'd be doing yourself
a disservice.

The layperson
versed in
Knowledge easy to recite.
Not quite
ready to bite
The Apple
of delight and fright
despite what might
occur.
The obscurity
of the unknown may lead to
Light or night.
Which is Right?

No one should speak
on areas that they,
themselves, are weak.
The ensuing hypocrisy
lends itself to deceit,
crafting an illusory image
as one holier than thee.

You know
yet act slow.
Truth in tow
but for show,
no?
Sow reaps no grow.
¡Cuidado!
before you throw
what's been bestowed.

Don't allow yourself to be led
by a less credible source.
Oh, the remorse
when you realize you've been
force-fed lead
and divorced
from the best possible Course.
Keep steadfast ahead
and tread seamlessly with The Force.

Many utter words premature.
I'd like to ensure
that what I posit is
matter-of-fact
integrity intact
not lackadaisically supposed
haphazardly composed
prose.
Better to be mute
than stutter half-truths
that can be easily disputed.
Absolutes cannot be refuted.

Don't heed the advice
of someone on speed.
Free yourself from the need
to seek reprieve externally.
The Eternal is the ultimate Voice,
capable of directing you
toward choices
that propel you forward
with minimal noise.

Being dependent on
someone or substance
has you feeling
lonesome and depressed,
which causes
unnecessary stress.
You can change that narrative.
It is imperative
that you don't regress.

The past
comes to disturb
my present,
its presence
- unwelcome -
feelings resurface
as if induced by
a recent cause.
My peace
now pieced apart
by hurt unresolved.

As pleasures surge,
curb the urge
to visit old tombs,
open scarred wounds
without consulting Reason.
Many come for a season
as a test.
One is encouraged
to progress
with less(ons).

Don't subscribe to bribery.
Being enticed by vices
is a surefire way to demise.
Suffer today
for a thriving tomorrow.
What a sorrow-filled life.
Don't consent to strife
before you find yourself
resent-ful.
Stifled by the flame
of an inhumane,
sadistic game.

Malevolent forces
cause my flesh such torment.
Feelings once dormant
erupt,
disrupting my calm.
My Spirit, a soothing balm.
My writing, a healing psalm
to quiet my writhing qualms.

People don't exist
until your gaze becomes fixated
on another.
Allow the memory to dissipate
with not an utter.
The bliss will be dearly missed
and subsequently dismissed
with no reminisce.
Smothered.
Go ghost;
become engrossed in
your own story
unlike most
who scroll mindlessly through posts
into an abysmal hole
with no end goal,
devoid of feeling whole.

Refrain from displacing blame
when you *knowingly*
stepped foot into the flame.
You had the foresight to avert pain.
Tame the lion's mane
before you defame your name.
Allow the temptation to wane
before the shame remains.

Through disciplinary action
one develops discipline
and strengthened intuition,
prompting one to listen
to the voice with-in
for any premonition.
Don't let causes affect (v.)
your affect (n.),
resulting in effects
that are difficult to neglect.
Eliminate the cause
and soon you'll find resolve.

Don't overcomplicate
the simplified.
In time
you'll learn
to discern
and refine
as you align
with The Divine
and mine
to the depths of the crystalline.

Don't move with haste
before you waste an opportunity
if not properly paced.
There's no race to be won.
Tread gracefully, knowing
there's nothing to be done.

It feels like déjà vu.
Thankfully,
I assume an aerial view,
so I can examine
my subjective objectively
with a perspective unskewed.

Picture this:
pressing matters take precedence,
and matters irrelevant
recede into the recesses
of my mind.
Purely afterthoughts,
residing in the hind.
Not at the forefront
of conscious perception,
trying to beckon
for my attention.
Either you grab ahold
of the reins and steer
or fold and veer
down a path unclear,
driven by impulses that reign supreme
while you remain passive
like passersby inactive.

Sever ties
with past li(v)es
before you meet
your inevitable demise.
No longer mesmerized
by impermanent highs.
Reside
in the all-knowing Eye,
Realized.